Activities for **3-5** year olds

Caring & Sharing

 Brilliant Publications   Janet Morris & Linda Mort

We hope you enjoy using this book. If you would like further information on other titles published by Brilliant Publications, please write to the address given below.

Published by Brilliant Publications, The Old School Yard, Leighton Road, Northall, Dunstable, Bedfordshire LU6 2HA

Written by Janet Morris and Linda Mort
Illustrated by Kirsty Wilson

Printed in Malta by Interprint Limited

Contents

Introduction

'Caring and sharing' is a very simple phrase to which young children readily respond. It sums up an approach to learning and to living with others which, if begun early enough, in a positive and enjoyable way, can carry a child through life.

The activities in this book are based on young children's needs for active learning and family involvement to reinforce the reciprocal values of home and school. They include ideas for encouraging children to enjoy using the words 'please' and 'thank you', to take turns, share, and to listen to one another. In this way, children are helped to appreciate kindness in others and to show kindness and respect for members of their own family, friends and the world around them.

The activities are organized to work within the framework of SCAA's Desirable Outcomes and take into account the child's developing intellectual, social and physical skills, focusing upon ideas that will encourage the growth of a positive self-image and a positive attitude towards those around him*.

Try to adopt a 'play' approach as much as possible, and be flexible. Whatever the focus of any activity, the children will be learning all kinds of things from it and much will depend on your starting point. Always start from what the children already know, and their interests. You should be able to adapt all the activities in this book to work with either individual children or a small group, without too much problem.

The book uses materials which are likely to be readily available within your class or group's location, or which can be easily gathered or collected from the children's families or carers.

To avoid the clumsy 'he/she', the child is referred to throughout as 'he'.

'Please' and 'thank you' bubbles

What children should learn

Language and literacy – to use the words 'please' and 'thank you' in conversation.

What you need

Card, felt-tipped pen, scissors, drinking straw, adhesive tape, play-people, miniature 'props' (eg furniture, small toys, 'shopping' items, etc), comics showing speech bubbles.

Activity

Make a card 'speech bubble', showing 'Please' on one side, and 'Thank you' on the reverse. Attach a drinking straw to make a flag. Show the children the speech bubbles in comics. Tell them they are going to help play-people to say 'please' and 'thank you' using their special 'speech bubble'. Give the speech bubble to one child and say that he must 'twirl' the 'bubble' to show the right word, whenever you use the words 'please' and 'thank you'. (Note: 'please' and 'thank you' are not as prominent in other languages and cultures.)

Select two play-people and a 'prop', and make up a very simple dialogue in which one play-person uses 'please' and the other 'thank you' (eg a child in bed, asking a parent for a drink). Let each child in turn make up a dialogue, with the child next to them twirling the 'bubble' appropriately.

Extension

Every child in the class could make a 'please and thank you bubble' to take home. Tell parents that everyone has been practising these words, and ask the parents to let you know how the children get on at home. Regularly report this feedback to the children!

Talk about

Who says, 'Tickets, please!', 'Open wide, please!', etc. How does it feel if people do not say 'thank you'?

Isn't that kind!

What children should learn

Language and literacy – to talk about their families in front of a group, and to describe one kind action.

What you need

Photographs of children's families.

Activity

Sit the children in a circle. Let them take turns to stand up, holding up photographs of their family, or the people they live with, for everyone to see. Ask them to say one kind action that daddy/mummy/brother/sister does for them and vice versa. For example, their big brother might help tie shoelaces whilst they might help find big brother's coat, etc.

Extension

Make little concertina booklets entitled 'Being kind' with the photograph the child has brought in on the front cover. The children can illustrate the pages with alternating pictures of the child being kind to a family member and a family member being kind to the child. Write captions to go with their illustrations.

Talk about

What makes members of your family pleased with you? What makes mummy and daddy smile? When do they say: 'What a good girl/boy?'.

I can help you

What children should learn

Language and literacy – to increase vocabulary and awareness of adult occupations, in particular, the 'caring professions'.

What you need

Pictures of people or animals needing help (eg a cat stuck up a tree, a child who has fallen off a bike, a child crying, lost in a crowd of adults), a firefighter's hat, a nurse's hat, a police hat, chairs, taped music.

Activity

Attach the pictures to the wall, a few feet apart ,within the children's reach. Ask three children at a time to dance around to the music wearing one of the hats. When the music stops the children should choose one of the pictures to go up to and say: 'I can help you'. Ask them to explain in more detail how they would help the animal/person in the picture.

Extension

Tell the classic tale of 'The Lion and the Mouse' in which the Lion first saves the Mouse's life and the Mouse is later able to help the Lion by gnawing through the hunter's rope. Explain that the story shows how we can all help each other in some way, however small.

Talk about

Ask whether any of the children have had contact with a nurse, police officer, firefighter, etc. How were they helped at the time?

Thank you!

What children should learn

Language and literacy – to use emergent writing to write thank you cards.

What you need

Paper, envelopes, stamps, felt-tipped pens, crayons, pencils, collage materials, glue, scissors.

Activity

Let the children think about people who could be thanked for their kindness and help – both those known personally to the children, and others. The children write cards or letters using their own level of emergent writing, with a 'scribe', if necessary. For example, one child could write a thank you card to granny, for taking him kite flying, or the whole class could make a giant card to say thank you to the cleaners, dinner helpers, caretaker, gardener, postperson, etc. The letters should be posted by the children.

Extension

Let the children pretend to be characters from stories or rhymes and write 'thank you' letters to people who were kind to them, updating their 'benefactors' with details of what happened to them after their meeting! Examples could be: Cinderella to the Fairy Godmother, Jack to the giant's wife, and Humpty to the 'all the King's horses and men' who tried to help him.

Talk about

How else can you say 'thank you' to people? (Hugs, kisses, presents, a good deed, etc.)

That's just like ...

What children should learn

Language and literacy – to empathize with characters they hear about in stories.

What you need

Stories (in books, or made up) about experiencing kindness from others, percussion instruments.

Activity

Choose key points from the story for the children to act out, perhaps to the accompaniment of percussion instruments. Change the characters and the setting. For example, if the story is about a child who is new to a playgroup, and feels lonely at first, the children could pretend to be a little squirrel who finds himself in a new forest, without any friends. Include one strong descriptive detail that also occurs in the story. For example, if in the story the little boy felt especially sad at playtime when it started to rain and all the other children ran inside, laughing, the squirrel could be feeling especially sad, lonely, shivering and cold when it starts to rain, and all the other squirrels dart off together, laughing, to find shelter.

A few hours later tell or read the actual story. Do not mention the earlier 'squirrel' experience. Let the children make their own connections.

Extension

Ask the children to talk about stories which reminded them of themselves, or people they know.

Talk about

When do they feel sad? Who cheers them up? How? How are they kind to people?

Shadow puppets

What children should learn

Language and literacy – to empathize with nursery rhyme characters who have hurt themselves.

What you need

A screen made out of a piece of white sheet fastened to a one metre square frame of wood or stiff card, a large torch or lamp, cut-out card nursery rhyme characters and props, attached to the ends of rulers or dowelling sticks, chairs.

Activity

Set out the chairs for the audience of children in front of the screen. Shine the light on the back of the screen. Holding up the cut-out characters behind the screen will make them appear as shadows on the screen. You or a child can take on the role of a nursery rhyme character needing help. For example, Humpty Dumpty could fall off the wall and the children could suggest ways of helping, eg gluing him back together.

Extension

The children could act out the nursery rhymes improvising their own solutions. For example, Jack might be taken to hospital in an ambulance rather than having his head wrapped in vinegar and brown paper!

Talk about

Which nursery rhyme characters need help from other people? What would the children do to help? Who helps them when they fall over? Are they upset?

The caring and sharing alphabet

What children should learn

Language and literacy – to match alphabet letters whilst developing vocabulary on a 'caring and sharing' theme.

What you need

An alphabet frieze, a set of alphabet letters, a drawstring bag.

Activity

Place the alphabet letters in the bag, and let one child choose a letter, say its sound and stand underneath the matching letter on the frieze. (The frieze could be laid on the floor.) The child then makes up a very simple 'caring and sharing' story involving the alphabet picture. For example, **a** – 'I shared my **a**pple with my sister'; **b** – 'I let my friend play with my new **b**all'; **n** – 'The **n**urse made the little girl better'; **z** – 'The **z**ebra picked up her friend when he fell in the mud', etc.

Extension

Let the children bring in their own alphabet books from home and make up 'caring and sharing' stories about the pictures contained in them.

Talk about

Who looks after the animals on the frieze? Do you have any toys like the ones on the frieze? Do you share them? Who gave them to you?

A handful of rings

What children should learn

Mathematics – to share out items equally between two people.

What you need

Plates, hoop-like crisps (you will need ten per child).

Activity

The children should wash their hands before doing this activity. Ask the children to sit on the floor, in pairs, facing one another, with a plate of ten 'hoops' between them. One child should hold up her outstretched fingers on one hand. The other child, 'the sharing child', should also hold up the fingers of one free hand. With the other hand he should pick up the 'hoops' one at a time and place one on one finger of the partner's hand, and then on one finger of his 'free' hand, saying each time, 'one for you, one for me', etc, until all ten 'hoops' are used up. The pair may then eat the 'hoops'. You should now replace the ten 'hoops', after which the other child can become the 'sharing' child.

Extension

Make a strip picture of six hands for the wall, showing the progression from an empty hand with no 'hoops', to a hand with five 'hoops'. Can the children match the numbers 0, 1, 2, 3, 4, 5, to the picture?

Talk about

Ask the children if they have noticed their parents sharing out the food when friends and relations visit. Do they give one item to each person? When cutting a cake, does everyone get the same size piece?

One peach each

What children should learn

Mathematics – to develop an understanding of sharing – 'one each'.

What you need

Salt dough made by mixing the following ingredients together to make a firm dough: 3 cups plain flour, 2 cups salt, 4 teaspoons wallpaper paste (without fungicide), 1 1/3 cups water. If more water is needed, add one drop at a time, kneading as you go. One fresh peach, one plastic plate, red and yellow powder paints, clear varnish, one die, one hoop.

Activity

Show the children a fresh peach, and let them make a quantity of 'pretend' peaches from salt dough. Bake in a very cool oven (70-100°C) for a minimum of 12 hours, turning occasionally. When cool, let the children paint the 'peaches', and varnish when dry. Place the 'peaches' on a plate on the floor inside the hoop. One child throws the die, and asks the corresponding number of children to sit around the circle. The child must then share out the 'peaches', one each. (Note:

make sure the children know that these are 'pretend peaches' and that they should not be eaten.)

Extension

Before each child shares the 'peaches', put differing amounts of 'peaches' on the plate, and ask the child to estimate whether there will be 'enough' for 'one each'. Let the child give 'two each', etc.

Talk about

Would it be fair for one child to keep all the peaches? If any peaches are 'left over', should some children have more than others? What could we do with the 'left over' peaches?

Make a queue and we'll get through!

What children should learn

Mathematics – to develop conservation of number in the context of a 'queue'.

What you need

Five play-people, three kitchen roll tubes, masking tape, scissors.

Activity

Make a narrow 'door-frame', using three kitchen roll tubes, cut to size. Secure the tubes using masking tape, and fix the 'door-frame' to a table, again with masking tape. Arrange the play-people side by side in a row in front of the 'door', and demonstrate that they cannot fit through the door all at once, when they are 'side by side'. Show that if they make a queue, 'one behind the other', then they will all get through the door. Keep counting the play-people, when they are side by side and when they are one behind the other, and point out that there are always five play-people and that they will all get through the door eventually.

Extension

Carry out the above procedure using the children themselves and a doorway. Before the children organize themselves into a queue let them say, 'Make a queue and we'll get through!'

Talk about

How many play-people want to get through the door? Can they all fit through the door at the same time when they are side by side? What would happen if they all tried to do this at once? What can the play-people do to stop themselves from getting hurt? For the extension activity ask: 'How many people are in the queue? Will they all get through the door? Does it matter who goes first? Why not?'

Giant piggy bank

What children should learn

Mathematics – to appreciate the concept of 'saving up' money collectively to buy an item which is shared by all.

What you need

A large plastic bottle, sharp scissors, a pipe-cleaner, card, felt-tipped pens, pretend money, adhesive tape, educational suppliers' or 'catalogue shop' catalogue, collection of piggy banks and money boxes.

Activity

Show the collection of piggy banks and money boxes and talk about 'saving up' to buy something special. Decide with the children on a special toy or item which could be bought by everyone, to share. Choose the item from one of the catalogues. Make a piggy bank by cutting a pig's face and legs from the card, and sticking them on to the bottle. Cut a slot in the top, and a larger flap underneath to retrieve the coins (tape this with adhesive tape for the moment). Add a curly tail made from a pipe cleaner. Let the children fill the piggy bank with pretend money. Point out how much more money is raised if everyone contributes.

Ideally arrange for the chosen toy or item to be bought at the next 'requisition'. (Note: if you have Muslim children who would be offended by references to pigs, you could substitute another animal.)

Extension

Whenever the children are raising money for charity, send a letter home about this. When the children/parents bring in a little money, let them put it in the transparent piggy bank.

Talk about

Who do the toys in the nursery/class belong to? Who looks after them? How do we share them and make sure they do not get lost and/or broken?

In five minutes

What children should learn

Mathematics – to develop a sense of how long 'five minutes' is and experience waiting for one's turn.

What you need

A plastic-fronted wall clock with a clear face, a decorative plate-stand, coloured peel-off labels.

Activity

Place the clock in the plate-stand and keep this in a known place, accessible for the children. Whenever one child wishes to use something being used by someone else, encourage the child to ask for a 'turn', and for the second child to say 'yes, in five minutes'. The first child should then bring the clock to you. Point out the 'big hand', and the next number it will move to, after five minutes. Place a coloured label by this number. The child may now take the clock and stand it up nearby, 'keeping an eye' on the time.

Extension

Use a three-minute egg-timer 'twice', to enable the children to appreciate 'waiting for a turn' for six minutes. Show the 'waiting child' how to turn the egg-timer after three minutes.

Talk about

What activity could the 'waiting child' could do in five or six minutes? For example, he could look at books, play with something else, sweep up the sand, etc.

Baby's bottle time

What children should learn

Mathematics – to develop early concepts of capacity in relation to filling babies' bottles.

What you need

Babies' feeding bottles, selection of baby dolls, jugs, cling film, white powder paint, water.

Activity

Mix a quantity of thin white powder paint, to represent 'milk'. (Explain to the children that this is 'pretend milk' and that people should not drink it.) Pour the 'milk' into jugs, and let the children carefully fill the bottles for their 'babies', trying not to spill any 'milk'. Ask them to guess how many bottles they can fill with the milk in the jug. When the 'feeds' are ready, use cling film and the bottles' discs, before adding the teats to prevent 'milk' leaking from the bottles.

Extension

Let the children have a dolls' tea party. Fill 'milk' jugs with powder-paint milk, and tea pots with cold tea. Ask the children to put the 'milk' in the cups either before or after the 'tea'.

Get the children to estimate when to stop pouring the tea or milk so there are no 'overflows'.

Talk about

Talk about how we have to look after babies, including feeding them carefully. Tell the children that most babies drink milk from their mothers' breasts, but that some of the time they may have bottles of milk. Talk about how babies of different sizes and weights need different amounts of milk, and how sometimes they will drink a whole bottle and sometimes only half. Point out the measurements on the bottles which indicate how many ounces or millilitres of milk the baby has drunk.

Shopping for baby

What children should learn

Mathematics – to develop matching and counting skills.

What you need

A large number of baby items (eg bottles, baby clothes, baby shampoo, boxes of wet wipes, rattles, nappies, etc), large piece of card, felt-tipped pen, pretend money, baby doll, baby catalogue and glue (optional).

Activity

On a large piece of card draw a picture of each baby item (or cut and paste pictures from a catalogue). Write the price alongside. Choose one child to be the mummy or daddy, complete with new 'baby'. Ask the other children to be the big 'brothers' and 'sisters', helping to buy items for the new baby, from the baby shop. Help the children to match the item they wish to buy with the picture or drawing on the card. Count how many items they have bought altogether. How many bottles? How many rattles?

Extension

Change the items in the shop, and go shopping for Christmas and birthday presents for relations and friends. Ask the children to think about what their relatives and friends like doing, and what they might like for a present.

Talk about

Discuss the needs of a new baby. How could children help to look after a new baby? If the children were to have a new baby in the family, what toy would they buy?

Caring and sharing week

What children should learn

Personal and social development – to share their own toys, and to 'take turns'.

What you need

Photocopier.

Activity

Send a letter home about 'Caring and sharing week', when each child may bring a toy/game to share with everyone else. Ask for the item to be labelled with the child's name and preferably not to have too many small parts. During the week, encourage each child to explain how to use his item. Encourage the children to ask for a 'turn' (see also *In five minutes*, page 16), and to use each other's items carefully.

Extension

Send home a letter asking parents/carers to jot down (on an enclosed form) any special 'caring and sharing' kind behaviour they see in their child, and to return the form during the 'caring and sharing week'. These notes could be read out at news or assembly time, especially if parents/carers are invited.

Talk about

Discuss how it is fun and interesting to share our belongings with others and how other people can give us new ideas for using our belongings. Ask the children what toys they share with their friends when they come to visit. What would happen if they did not share their toys?

Word traffic

What children should learn

Personal and social development – to take turns when speaking in a small group.

What you need

A set of numbers (one each), card, saucer, felt-tipped pen, scissors, orange, green and red sticky paper, adhesive tape, police hat.

Activity

Cut one saucer-sized circle out of card per child. Stick orange sticky paper on one side, and green on the reverse. Cut out one larger circle and make this red on both sides. Give each child a number and a circle, to put on the table in front of them. The circles should be 'orange' side up. Tell the children that when people talk in a group they must listen to one another and not interrupt. The child who is speaking may turn his circle over to show 'green'. Everyone else must listen, and think about what they might like to say when it is their turn. They should not speak, but be 'getting ready' (like a car at traffic lights). When their turn comes, they turn their circle over to 'green', and may then speak.

Choose one child to be a police officer, who wears the hat, and holds the large red circle. The 'police officer' must hold up the red circle to stop any child who interrupts.

You should begin a discussion, then the child with number '1' may then turn his circle over to green, and say something. When he is finished it is number 2's turn, etc.

Extension

Once the children are used to taking turns, try without the numbers. Emphasize that everyone will get a turn!

Talk about

What happens when everyone tries to talk at once? What would happen to traffic if there were no traffic lights?

Can I help you?

What children should learn

Personal and social development – to help each other in a practical way and to develop awareness of their own capabilities.

What you need

Children's outdoor clothing (eg coats, anoraks, gloves, scarves, hats, etc).

Activity

Put the children in pairs just before an outdoor playtime and ask them to bring their coats, etc. Tell them that instead of asking an adult for help with zips, buttons, etc, they should be 'just like grown-ups' and see if they can help each other to put on their clothes.

Extension

Make a pictogram (a bar chart with pictures) showing how many children have coats with buttons, compared with those with zips or press studs. You could also make a pictogram to compare numbers of gloves and mittens.

Talk about

What sort of clothes are the most difficult to put on? Can the children put one hand on top of one of their gloves, and match each of their fingers to a glove finger? Can they do this with a mitten, 'bunching up' four fingers together? How can they tell a right boot or shoe from the left one? (Suggest that if they put them side by side, and the toes are pointing away from one another, then the shoes 'don't want to be friends' and are the wrong way around!)

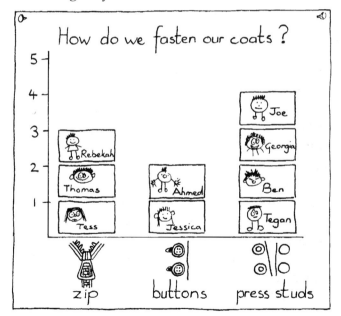

Get well soon!

What children should learn

Creative development – to use a range of materials to make a 'get well' card for a sick friend.

What you need

Card, felt-tipped pens, toy catalogues, scissors, a child who is off sick(!), cassette tape recorder.

Activity

Sit the children in a circle and chat to them about the sick child's favourite toys, stories and activities. Ask them what they think he might miss, not being at nursery/school/playgroup. The children can draw pictures or cut out pictures from catalogues of the sick child's favourite toys/stories/activities. Make the children's pictures into a collage on a large piece of folded card. Help the children write a get well message inside with the younger children 'writing' lots of brightly coloured kisses!

Extension

Make a 'cheer-up' tape for the sick child by letting each child record a short message saying what they would like to do with the child when he returns to nursery/school/playgroup.

Talk about

Have the children ever received get well cards? Did it make them feel happy? What activities could they do at home when they are not feeling too well? Duplo? Jigsaws? Painting?

Look inside

What children should learn

Creative development – to sing the following song (to the tune of 'Baa Baa Black Sheep'):

Brown hair, black hair, ginger hair or blond,
Blue eyes, green eyes, brown or grey,
People may look different on the outside,
but inside they feel just like you!

What you need

Large piece of card, felt-tipped pens.

Activity

On the card draw a row of four vertical ovals, with brown, black, ginger and blond hair respectively. Do not draw facial features on the ovals. Beneath the ovals draw four pairs of large eyes – blue, green, brown and grey. Ask the children to hum the tune of 'Baa Baa Black Sheep', and then teach the words of the song, pointing to the appropriate hair and eye colours as you sing.

Extension

Ask the children for ideas for other words that could be substituted in the song (eg curly hair, straight hair, long legs, short legs, different clothes, etc).

Talk about

Talk about how people all over the world look different 'on the outside' (different features and clothes), and how this makes a colourful and interesting world. Explain how 'outside' differences do not matter, and are not important. Say that we all have the same feelings 'on the inside' and should all be kind to one another, otherwise people's feelings can be hurt. Ask the children to talk about times when they, or a friend, have had their feelings hurt, and about what we can all do to cheer someone up to whom this has happened.

Forgetful Ferdinand

What children should learn

Physical development – to understand and follow instructions for physical activities.

What you need

A space for the children.

Activity

Initially, you should be 'Forgetful Ferdinand', who 'often forgets to say "please"'. Give the children instructions to follow, as in 'Simon says', but for all actions you wish them to follow, say 'Ferdinand says please …'. The children must not carry out any instruction which does not include the word 'please'. This is a good activity to help develop spatial awareness, eg 'Ferdinand says please stand behind your chair' or 'Ferdinand says please sit under the climbing frame.'

Extension

Extend the game to a shopping context, by playing 'Ferdinand forgets to say thank you!', with Ferdinand asking to buy something from the 'shopkeeper'.

Carry out the role play with you as Ferdinand and one child as the shopkeeper, in front of the rest of the group. The shopkeeper gives the item to Ferdinand who forgets to say 'thank you'. The shopkeeper takes the item back, saying: 'What do you say?'. Ferdinand says: 'Sorry, I've forgotten! What do I say, children?' Let the group remind Ferdinand!

Talk about

Do the children know anyone who forgets to say 'please' and 'thank you'? (Perhaps a younger brother or sister whom they can help teach?!)

'Excuse me!' and 'Sorry!'

What children should learn

Physical development – to ride a tricycle with increasing skill and confidence.

What you need

A large space, a group of six children, a firefighter's hat, a police hat, an ambulance worker's hat, five chairs, placed one behind each other in a row, with plenty of space in between, one tricycle.

Activity

Five children sit on the chairs and pretend to be 'traffic driving along'. The sixth child can choose to be the driver of a fire engine, police car or ambulance, and puts on the appropriate hat. This child is allowed to weave in and out of the chairs on the tricycle, 'overtaking', while using his 'siren voice', repeating the expression 'excuse me! excuse me! excuse me!' (instead of 'der ... der! der ... der! der ... der!'). If the tricycle touches a chair, the emergency driver must say 'sorry!'. The children should take turns being the emergency driver.

Extension

Let five children stand one behind the other, with a space between each child. Tell the children to pretend that they have very heavy shopping bags, and have stopped for a moment to have a little rest. Let the sixth child pretend to be in a hurry. This child must hurry in and out of the standing children, but must say 'excuse me!' each time. If he bumps into a standing child, he must say 'sorry!'.

Talk about

Tell the children that a siren on emergency vehicle means: 'Excuse me, I'm in a hurry, please let me pass!'. Talk about how drivers of emergency vehicles often need to drive very quickly, but that they always take care not to crash into any other traffic. Explain that if emergency vehicles or any traffic do bump into each other then everyone is very sorry indeed.

TO 27259

Grow a green pepper plant

What children should learn

Knowledge and understanding of the world – to grow a plant from seed and what plants need to grow.

What you need

Plastic cups, potting compost, green peppers, sharp knife, water, peel off labels, felt-tipped pen, plastic spoons.

Activity

Let each child fill a cup with compost. Stick a name label on each cup. Cut the green peppers in half and let the children remove the seeds. Ask each child to sprinkle a few seeds on the compost. Add a top layer of compost and then a little water. (Note: the children should wash their hands thoroughly afterwards as pepper seeds can sometimes cause irritation if they come in contact with the eyes or mouth.)

Let each child take their cup home, with instructions to keep the compost moist. The seeds will start to grow in a matter of days and luxuriant plants will appear in a few weeks. Ask the children to bring their plants back to show everyone.

Extension

Let the children try planting red or yellow pepper seeds, too.

Talk about

Explain how we need to feel the compost each day to see if the plant needs watering. Talk about why the plant needs light to help it grow.

Share a bath!

What children should learn

Knowledge and understanding of the world – to appreciate the importance of water conservation as part of caring for our world.

What you need

Two dolls, two baby baths, bubble bath, waterproof aprons, large jug, face cloths, towels.

Activity

Ask the children to undress the dolls ready for a bath. Place the one bath and a jug of warm water in front of the children. Give the children a problem to solve. Tell them : 'We don't want to waste water as it is precious, but we do want to bath both dolls'. Ask them what they think you should do. Most children will realize that the two dolls can both be bathed together in one bath. Pour the jug of water into the bath, add the bubble bath, and let the children enjoy washing the dolls clean.

Extension

The children could collect water in a water butt or buckets when it rains, and use this to water plants.

Talk about

Discuss all the different uses of water in everyday life for washing, drinking, cooking, brushing teeth, growing plants, etc. Explain how, when there is not much rain, it is especially important not to waste water, so that there will be enough for everyone, eg by sharing baths or showers, always putting plugs in sinks, etc.

Walk in the dark

What children should learn

Knowledge and understanding of the world – to observe the night-time environment as they help one another in the dark.

What you need

Warm clothing, one torch for every pair of children, a duplicated letter sent to parents, a winter day, coloured cellophane, adhesive tape, extra adults to help supervise the activity.

Activity

Send a letter home informing parents that the children are invited to go on a late afternoon winter's walk. (Some parents might like to accompany the children.) Attach fluorescent stripes to the children's clothes with adhesive tape. Shine a torch on the stripes so that the children can see how they show up in the dark. Discuss the importance of being seen by traffic.

Divide the children into pairs and give each pair a torch. Make sure each adult knows which pair(s) of children he or she is supervising. Walk around the local streets with the children taking turns to use the torch.

Extension

Experiment with covering the torch with coloured cellophane to make everything appear red/green/blue, etc.

Talk about

What would happen if they could not see where they were walking? Do they know anyone who is blind? What sounds can the children hear? What animals/ birds come out at night?

Rubbish gobblers

What children should learn

Knowledge and understanding of the world – to design and make a small litter bin for their bedroom.

What you need

Large pieces of card, felt-tipped pens, paints, crayons, collage items (eg wool, bottle tops, etc), glue, scissors, hole punch, string, parcel tape, rulers, tape measures, plastic-coated wire, photocopier.

Activity

Over a period of a few weeks, send a letter home with a small group of children at a time, asking each child to bring in a small cardboard box. Tell the children they are going to turn their box into a special 'rubbish gobbler' litter bin to keep their bedrooms tidy. They can choose whatever creature they want for their bin (eg lion, tiger, monster, robot, etc). Let each child make a 'rubbish gobbler' face on a piece of card. Talk to them about how big their piece of card will need to be, and help them to cut out a large mouth, through which the rubbish will be 'fed'. Discuss with each child the best way of attaching the card to their bin (eg string, parcel tape, plastic coated wire).

Extension

Ask for ideas for transforming the classroom bins into 'rubbish gobblers'. Take votes on the most popular suggestions, and involve all the children in designing the faces for them.

Talk about

Do the children keep their rooms tidy? How? What sort of rubbish will they put in their 'rubbish gobblers'? What would happen if we did not have litter bins?

'Come aboard'

What children should learn

Knowledge and understanding of the world – to work cooperatively to build a big bus.

What you need

Large construction set with nuts, bolts and wheels, paper, felt-tipped pens, adhesive tape.

Activity

This activity works best with a group of five or six children. Ask the children to work together to create a bus for a special trip to the seaside. Practise screwing and unscrewing the nuts and bolts. Put each child in charge of one part of the construction set: nuts, bolts, wheels, cubes, etc, so that the children have to work cooperatively asking each other for the part they need. When the bus is finished, the children can draw their faces with felt-tipped pens on squares of paper to represent faces at the windows.

Extension

Sing 'The Wheels on the Bus' song changing the words to include individual children eg. 'Lauren on the bus has a sister called Isabel' ...

Talk about

Tell the children how in car and bus factories people work together in 'teams', all helping one another. Talk about sports teams, such as football teams, where the players have to kick the ball to one another and not keep the ball to themselves.

Kind children book

What children should learn

Knowledge and understanding of the world – to develop an awareness of family history.

What you need

Paper, crayons, large sheets of sugar paper, glue, long-armed stapler, adhesive tape, photocopier.

Activity

Send a letter home, asking parents, carers and grandparents to write down (on an enclosed form) a short anecdote about a kind deed which they carried out when they were small. When the forms are returned, ask the children to illustrate them, and stick the original forms and pictures in a large sugar paper book, entitled 'Kind children'. Photographs of the children's parents and grandparents (as children) could also be sent in. Photocopies of these could be included in the 'Kind children' book.

Extension

Have a special time each day when everyone, children and staff, can talk about anyone who has been kind to them that day.

Talk about

Do the children know the names of their aunts and uncles, and that they are the brothers and sisters of their parents? How are the children kind to their brothers and sisters? How are their brothers and sisters kind to them?

Around the world week

What children should learn

Knowledge and understanding of the world – to foster feelings of mutual respect for people all around the world.

What you need

Word processor, photocopier, globe or map of the world, display table and board.

Activity

Send a letter home about your 'Around the world week'. Ask parents to write down (on an enclosed form) a favourite, simple recipe (that the children could make), or simple game, story, song, anecdote or joke from anywhere in the world (with explanatory details, if necessary). During the week, play the games, sing the songs and tell the stories. Make the recipes and have tasting sessions for everyone at going home time.

Extension

The parents' contributions could be made into an 'Around the world' booklet, to be sold to raise money for a children's charity.

Involve the children in designing a display table for the booklets based on ideas the parents have sent in. If possible, invite a representative from your chosen children's charity to talk to your children about how the money they are raising from the sale of their booklet will help others.

Talk about

Have the children ever visited another place for a holiday or had visitors to stay from another country? Can they bring postcards and items for the 'Around the world' display?